God is love; and he that dwelleth in love dwelleth in God, and God in him.

1 John 4:16

Pathways

Thou wilt shew me the path of life.

Psalms 16:11

Pathways

Compiled by

Jo Petty

The C.R. Gibson Company

Norwalk, Connecticut

The material in this book has
been collected over a long period
of time. Many of the original
sources are unknown to the compiler.
The compiler wishes to acknowledge
the original authors, whoever they
may be, but has confidence that
they would urge, with her, "Do not
inquire as to who said this, but
pay attention to what is said."

Walking
in the
Way of Love

 *Love*

The cure for all the ills and wrongs, the sorrows
and the crimes of humanity all lie in the one word,
"LOVE." It is the divine vitality that everywhere
produces and restores life; each and every one
of us has the power of working miracles if we
truly love.

When I speak of love, I mean the love which loves
because of its own inherent nature, not because of
the existence or worth of its object — spontaneous,
automatic love.

> Could we judge all deeds by motives,
> See the good and bad within,
> Surely we would love the sinner,
> All the while we loathe the sin.

God has taught us all truth in teaching us to love.

A person who always loves never seems to grow
old since so many charms are preserved.

Home is where love is best taught and learned.

To be a Christian does not mean that I have
arrived, but that I am on my way!

I am the only me, and God loves me!

If the tender, profound, and sympathizing love
practiced and recommended by Jesus were
paramount in every heart, the loftiest and most
glorious idea of human society would be realized.

The education of the soul for eternity should begin
and be carried on at the fireside.

Life is but one continual course of instruction — we
can learn something from every person we meet.
But our parents are our first church and school.
The parents write on the heart of the child the first
faint characters which time deepens into strength
so that nothing can efface them.

Let love be without dissimulation. Abhor that which
is evil; cleave to that which is good.

Romans 12:9

I still sing one of the very first songs I learned
as a child:

> Jesus loves me!
> This I know
> For the Bible tells me so.

Having learned that Jesus loves me, I consider this
the greatest lesson anyone can learn.

O yes, it is better to have a house without a roof
than a family unsheltered by God's love and the
feeling of not being always at rest in His
providential care.

God has ordered that, being in need of each other,
we should learn to love each other and bear one
another's burdens.

 *Love*

Love is the greatest thing that God can give us, for He Himself is Love; and it is the greatest thing we can give to God. The apostles call it the bond of perfection (*See Colossians 3:14*); it is the old, the new, and the great commandment, for it is the fulfilling of the law. (*See Romans 13:10.*) It does the work of all the other graces without any instrument but its own immediate virtue.

Love is the living essence of the Divine Nature which beams full of goodness.

If I truly love, I have God in me, for God is Love.

(See I John 4:7.)

True love is eternal, infinite, and always like itself.

Love forgives.

Do not complicate what Jesus has made clear enough for a child to comprehend about forgiveness. To be forgiven by God, we must forgive all who offend us.

Forgiveness is release.

Forgiveness is reconciliation.

Forgiveness is a new beginning.

For if ye forgive men their trespasses, your heavenly Father will also forgive you: But if ye forgive not men their trespasses, neither will your Father forgive your trespasses.

Matthew 6:14-15

And though I have the gift of prophecy, and understand all mysteries, and all knowledge; and though I have all faith, so that I could remove mountains, and have not love, I am nothing.

(See I Corinthians 13:2.)

The Bible teaches that if I confess my sins to God, He will forgive me just like my mother would kiss my disobedient acts into everlasting oblivion. *(See I John 1:9.)* Then my sins are as far away as the east is from the west.

(See Psalms 103:12.)

Do not rehash something God has refused to remember.

(See Isaiah 43:25.)

Love founded on true virtue never dies.

Love is wisdom.

Lie down on the bosom of God's infinite love.

The Lord hath appeared of old unto me, saying, Yea, I have loved thee with an everlasting love: therefore with lovingkindness have I drawn thee.

Jeremiah 31:3

Love is power.

Smiling is love.

Love gives itself, it is not bought.

Love one human being purely and warmly and you will love all.

9

Love

True love always finds a way to communicate.

If I neglect my love for my neighbor, in vain do I profess my love for God.

(See Matthew 22:37, 39.)

Remember the story of the two bears? Bear and forbear.

Let brotherly love continue.

Hebrews 13:1

Love is happier in the happiness of another than in its own happiness.

Mutual love is the crown of all our bliss.

Like sunlight through a prism, love breaks into many parts.

Love suffers long when necessary.

Love is ever kind.

Love does not envy.

Love does not exalt itself.

Love seeks not its own.

Love never fails.

A friend loveth at all times.

Proverbs 17:17

And when we know we are loved by God Himself
far more than any human is capable of loving us,
we can be so filled with His love that we can teach
love to others. All the king's horses and all the
king's men cannot make us love, but God can give
us a heart capable of loving.

> God's love is in the sunshine's glow,
> His life is in the quickening air,
> When lightnings flash and storm winds blow,
> There is His power; His law is there.

> God of the earth, the sky, the sea,
> Maker of all things above, below,
> Creation lives and moves in Thee,
> Your present life through all does flow.

The Lord's hand is not shortened, that it cannot
save; neither His ear heavy, that it cannot hear:
But my iniquities have separated me from God, and
my sins have caused Him to hide His face from me
so that He will not hear me when I call upon Him.

(See Isaiah 59:1-2.)

For a small moment God has forsaken me, but with
great mercies will He receive me. In a little wrath
He hid His face from me for a moment; but with
everlasting kindness will He have mercy on me. So
says the Lord, my Redeemer.

(See Isaiah 54:7-8.)

God has no other child like me. I am unique. I have
a beauty all my own.

 *Love*

Obedience to God is the most infallible evidence of
a sincere and supreme love for Him.

Love one another: for he that loveth another hath
fulfilled the law.

Romans 13:8

All our loves are fed from the fountain of
Infinite Love.

Love is not an art — it is life.

A little girl went into the cathedral during the week
when it was empty. When she came out, she was
asked what she did while in there. She replied,
"Oh, I just loved God a little."

Life is an education in His love.

We are successful if we have learned to love.

And above all things have fervent charity among
yourselves: for charity shall cover the multitude
of sins.

I Peter 4:8

Now the God of hope fill you with all joy and peace.

Romans 15:13

Walking in the
Way of
Joy and Peace

Joy and Peace

Surely the happiest word in the whole language is "whosoever"!

When the Lord said "whosoever" He included me!

> I am so glad that our Father in heaven
> Tells of His love in the book He has given.
> Wonderful things in the Bible I see —
> This is the dearest — Jesus loves me!

The elect are whosoever will. The non-elect are whosoever won't.

Jesus did not say that at the end of the way you shall find Me. He said, "I am the way!" *(See John 14:6.)* Happiness is not a station where you arrive — it is a matter of traveling.

Jesus taught us a wonderful secret: seek first the kingdom of God and His righteousness, and all the lesser things which make us happy will be added.

(See Luke 12:31.)

Every day is a good day, though some seem to be better than others.

I shall speak to myself in psalms and hymns and spiritual songs, singing and making melody in my heart to the Lord; giving thanks always for all things unto God the Father in the name of my Lord Jesus Christ.

(See Ephesians 5:19.)

I shall bid myself a good day today.

Youth ought to plant all provisions for a long and happy life.

Our Creator endowed us with the right to create happiness for ourselves and others.

God has given us wit, and flavor, and brightness and laughter to enliven the days of our pilgrimage.

Lo, Jesus is with me always, even unto the end of the world!

(See Matthew 28:20.)

There are too many joys for me to ever call this life a valley of tears though there are tears in it.

O the joy of the game of life! Let me keep a childlike appetite for what is coming next!

To make knowledge valuable, we must have the cheerfulness of wisdom.

Whatsoever things are true, whatsoever things are honest, whatsoever things are just, whatsoever things are pure, whatsoever things are lovely, whatsoever things are of good report; if there be any virtue, and if there be any praise, think on these things.

Philippians 4:8

Love life and feel the value of it.

There is no way of living joyfully without living justly.

 *Joy and Peace*

The fear of the Lord is a fruitful garden.

Wisdom will feed him that fears the Lord with the bread of understanding, and he shall be given the water of wisdom to drink, and he shall find joy and gladness.

There is nothing better than the fear of the Lord and there is nothing sweeter than to take heed unto the commandments of the Lord.

The fear of the Lord is wisdom and instruction: and faith and meekness are His delight.

The Word of God most high is the fountain of wisdom.

If I am trusting in the Lord, I am happy.

I live in pleasure only when I live in God.

God made me for Himself, for His pleasure. He moves me to delight in praising Him.

If I delight myself in the Lord, He shall give me the desires of my heart.

(See Psalms 37:4.)

The beauty all about us is God's handwriting.

Life, if properly viewed in all aspects, is great.

Jesus said that it is more blessed to give than to receive.

(See Acts 20:35.)

A Mother's Prayer

With a heart that was pure, and an eye seeing
    clear,
She looked on a world full of woe,
And begged with a woman's passionate might,
"Dear Father, O pray let me go.

"I will use all the strength of my earnest soul
To teach them the way to Thee."
But the Father but drew her more close unto Him,
And answered her passionate plea:

"I have many a voice that is loud and strong
To speak to the world for me,
But I've no one to sing a lullaby song
To this wee little babe but thee."

And the song was so sweet, and the song was
    so soft,
That the babe on her bosom smiled,
And the world that was weary of noise and
    of strife
Saw God in the mother and child.

Eleanor Scott Sharples

I have great duties and great songs.

A duty well performed is a great joy.

With thee is the fountain of life.

Psalms 36:9

Joy and Peace

The unrest of this weary world is the unvoiced cry after God.

I can live a beautiful life in my present circumstances.

God gives us richly all things to enjoy. *(See I Timothy 6:17.)* Knowing this makes and keeps me happy.

Thankfulness and cheerfulness reflect the gracious light of God's countenance.

Count your blessings. You shall soon be on your knees praising the Lord for all His goodness to you.

May all your seen pleasures lead to the unseen Fountain from which they flow.

Every good gift and every perfect gift is from above, and cometh down from the Father of lights, with whom is no variableness, neither shadow of turning.

James 1:17

I can be glad in all conditions and events, knowing God is in control.

That which is born of trust in God rises into rapture. God gives joy in sorrow. We can sing through our tears.

My inward joy is independent of my circumstances.

No one can take away my joy which God gives me.

(See John 16:22.)

Joy and Peace

If I fail to hear God's voice, it is not because He is not speaking to me, but because I am not listening. I must be quiet to hear the still, small voice of God.

(See I Kings 19:12.)

When the world seems dark and cold to me, I am the reason.

I sought the Lord, and he heard me, and delivered me from all my fears.

Psalms 34:4

If on a quiet sea toward heaven we calmly sail,
With grateful hearts, O God, to Thee,
We'll own the favoring gale,
But should the surges rise, and rest delay to come,
Blest be the tempest, kind the storm
Which drives us nearer home.

Prayer: Give me the calm beauty of an ordered life, whose every breath is praise to God.

Order contributes to peace in the home. A place for everything and everything in its place is a wonderful rule.

We do not keep the outward form of order if there is deep distress in the mind.

There is no real joy unless we have peace. The closer we draw to God (He draws us to Him), the more peaceful we become.

 *Joy and Peace*

In the keeping of God's commandments are great rewards, and peace is only one of them.

We are not immune to difficulties, but we can have peace in difficulties.

How comforting to feel I am in the very niche God ordained for me to fill.

I thank God for His wing of love which stirred my worldly nest, and for the stormy clouds which drove me, trembling to His breast.

> Drop Thy still dews of quietness
> Till all my strivings cease
> Let sense be dumb, let flesh retire,
> Speak through the earthquake, wind and fire,
> Thy still small voice of calm.

I shall not bear tomorrow's load of care. I shall not weep over yesterday. I shall leave the past and the present and the future with God.

And the work of righteousness shall be peace; and the effect of righteousness quietness and assurance for ever.

Isaiah 32:17

> O give Thine own sweet rest to me,
> That I may speak with soothing power
> A word in season, as from Thee,
> To weary ones in needful hour.

Joy and Peace

No real peace can abide with the person who lives contrary to the Word of God.

Quiet minds cannot be perplexed or frightened but go on in fortune or in misfortune at their own private pace, like the ticking of a clock during a thunderstorm.

Trust ye in the Lord for ever: for in the Lord Jehovah is everlasting strength.

Isaiah 26:4

Oh that I may trust in the Lord with all my heart and lean not to my own understanding.

(See Proverbs 3:5.)

Fear God and all other fears will disappear.

> Stilled now be every anxious care,
> See God's great goodness everywhere;
> Leave all to Him in perfect rest;
> He will do all things for the best.

For I the Lord thy God will hold thy right hand, saying unto thee, Fear not; I will help thee.

Isaiah 41:13

The more perfect my self-surrender, the more perfect my peace.

Ye shall find rest unto your souls.

Matthew 11:29

 *Joy and Peace*

Say "yes" to God's will. Lie quietly under His hand, having no will but His.

Peace may be the highest result of power. In quietness and confidence shall be my strength.

(See Isaiah 30:15.)

Peace is reconciliation with God and conscience.

Nothing is worth the loss of my peace.

The Word of God breathes sweet peace, joy and love into our hearts.

I desire nothing, reject nothing; all that God wills for me I joyfully accept I tell Him to pay no attention to me if ever I pray for anything outside His will, and I have great peace.

I believe that I have laid aside all self-seeking and all self-will. How else can I explain this marvellous peace within?

People who are serene and peaceful due to their walk with God never lose their beauty.

When I take one step away from God, I am a mile from the gates of peace.

While conscience is my friend, I am at peace. If I offend this friend, I am no longer at peace but troubled, fearful and anxious.

Be still, and know that I am God.

Psalms 46:10

I must learn to be contented with what happens, for what God chooses is better than what I would choose.

Thou wilt keep him in perfect peace, whose mind is stayed on thee: because he trusteth in thee.

Isaiah 26:3

Love plus forgiveness equals peace.

It is vain for me to expect, it is impudent for me to ask God's forgiveness for myself if I refuse to exercise a forgiving temper toward another.

For my thoughts are not your thoughts, neither are your ways my ways, saith the Lord. For as the heavens are higher than the earth, so are my ways higher than your ways, and my thoughts than your thoughts.

Isaiah 55:8,9

If I follow the admonitions of Jesus, I shall not permit my heart to be troubled *(see John 14:1)*. In coming to Him for help, I shall be at rest, and I shall not fret myself while waiting on the Lord. I shall follow His leading beside the still waters.

(See Psalms 23:2.)

Peace does not dwell in outward things but within ourselves. We may have peace in disagreeable things if we yield ourselves to the Prince of Peace.

Joy and Peace

Oh how great is God's goodness which He has laid up for them that fear Him; which He has wrought for them that trust in Him before men! He will hide them in the secret of His presence from the pride of man, He shall keep them secretly from the strife of tongues.

(See Psalms 31:19,20.)

The world is not in chaos. An acorn will still produce an oak, not an elm, and the ducks still fly south at the same time, and the swallow still arrives on time at Capistrano. People without Christ are in chaos. It is Christ or chaos.

In Christ are hid all the treasures of wisdom and knowledge.

(See Colossians 2:3.)

Let us hear the conclusion of the whole matter: Fear God, and keep His commandments: for this is the whole duty of man.

Ecclesiastes 12:13

Peace I leave with you, my peace I give unto you: not as the world giveth, give I unto you. Let not your heart be troubled, neither let it be afraid.

John 14:27

Blessed be the Lord: for he hath
shewed me his marvellous kindness.

Psalms 31:21

Walking in the
Way of
Goodness and Kindness

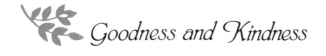 *Goodness and Kindness*

The great acts of love are done by those who are habitually performing small acts of kindness.

Pleasant words are as an honeycomb, sweet to the soul, and health to the bones.

Proverbs 16:24

Nothing multiplies so much as kindness.

Kind feelings make noble the smallest act.

The luxury of doing kindnesses surpasses every other personal enjoyment.

Kindness is taught by precept and example.

Kindness will convert more sinners than will zeal, eloquence or learning.

If thine enemy be hungry, give him bread to eat; and if he be thirsty, give him water to drink.

Proverbs 25:21

Give kind looks. Do kind acts and don't forget the warm handshakes.

Giving all diligence, add to your faith virtue; and to virtue knowledge; And to knowledge temperance; and to temperance patience; and to patience godliness; And to godliness brotherly kindness; and to brotherly kindness charity.

II Peter 1:5-7

Politeness comes from within, from the heart.

Goodness and Kindness

Politeness is benevolence in small things.

Politeness of the heart is akin to love.

Politeness says, "I would make you happy."

Follow after righteousness, godliness, faith, love, patience, meekness.

I Timothy 6:11

Courtesies of a small nature strike deep to the grateful heart.

It is kindness in a person, not beauty, which wins our love.

Pray for a short memory of all unkindness.

Don't speak of others' faults until you have none of your own.

The words of a wise man's mouth are gracious.

Ecclesiastes 10:12

Be courteous to everyone.

Charity suffereth long, and is kind.

I Corinthians 13:4

A pleasant smile accomplishes wonders.

A man that hath friends must shew himself friendly.

Proverbs 18:24

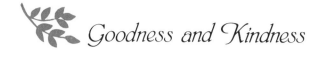 *Goodness and Kindness*

Let your conversation be as it becometh the gospel of Christ.

Philippians 1:27

The desire of a man is his kindness.

Proverbs 19:22

Do today's duty today.

No person can really be strong, gentle, pure and good, without the world being better for it, without somebody being helped and comforted by the very existence of his or her kindness.

Let every one of us please his neighbour for his good to edification.

Romans 15:2

My vocation is the simple round of duties which the passing hour brings.

The post of honor is the path of duty.

Duty by habit turns into pleasure.

It is my duty to be kind to all who cross my path.

There is a noble forgetfulness — that which does not remember injuries.

The bigger the heart, the less room for the memory of a wrong.

Labor is rest from the sorrows that greet us; from all the petty vexations that meet us.

Not with sword's loud clashing
Nor roll of stirring drums,
With deeds of love and mercy
The heavenly kingdom comes.

Be kindly affectioned one to another with brotherly
love; in honour preferring one another.

Romans 12:10

It is hard for the face to conceal the thoughts of
the heart.

Learn the art of mixing gentleness with firmness. It
is better to have headaches for rebuking when
necessary than to have heartaches later.

A word or even a nod from one who loves us
carries a lot of weight.

O, for homes ruled according to God's Word!

Our chief wisdom consists in knowing our follies
and faults, so that we may correct them.

I take great comfort in the statement that nobody is
perfect and that I am the perfect example.

The merciful man doeth good to his own soul: but
he that is cruel troubleth his own flesh.

Proverbs 11:17

Be kind to yourself!

Share your joy if you wish to have more.

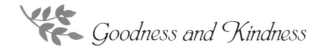

Goodness and Kindness

How lovely are the faces of
Those who talk with God . . .
Lit with an inner sureness of
The path their feet have trod;
How gentle is the manner of
Those who walk with Him!

He that doeth good is of God.

III John 11

Teach me Thy patience; still with Thee
In closer, dearer company,
In work that keeps faith sweet and strong,
In trust that triumphs over wrong.

Let us not be weary in well doing: for in due season
we shall reap.

Galatians 6:9

I can be kind in looks, words and acts.

Blessed be the Lord: for he hath shewed me his
marvellous kindness.

Psalms 31:21

Combat another's anger with a smile and a
kind word.

If I take a good look at myself, I will learn to look at
others differently.

Above all, put on charity, which is the bond
of perfectness.

(See Colossians 3:14.)

Goodness and Kindness

Forbearing one another, and forgiving one another,
if any man have a quarrel against any: even as
Christ forgave you, so also do ye.

Colossians 3:13

When I have failed to be the kind person I should
be, I pray that my failure may cause someone to
want to behave differently. Sometimes I think I may
have learned more tolerance from the intolerant
than the tolerant. I ask God to take all my failures
and somehow, somewhere, sometime, make them
show forth His praise.

Kindness to children and a willingness to conform
to the ideal character of childhood are the marks
of a true Christian.

For the mountains shall depart, and the hills be
removed; but my kindness shall not depart from
thee, neither shall the covenant of my peace be
removed, saith the Lord that hath mercy on thee.

Isaiah 54:10

Prayer
O fill me with Thy fulness, Lord,
Until my very heart o'erflow
In kindling thought and glowing word,
Thy love to tell, Thy praise to show.

A merry heart doeth good like a medicine.

Proverbs 17:22

# Goodness and Kindness

The true ornament of any person is virtue, not clothes or jewels.

Goodness heightens beauty.

Much knowledge will not benefit me if I am not honest.

Jesus is the foundation of my hopes, the object of my faith, and the subject of my love. He is the model for my conduct.

When my son asked, "What do you want me to be when I grow up?" I replied, "A good man."

Even the best of people make mistakes. But we can learn good through evil and progress to goodness and greatness through great mistakes. If my family were perfect, I could not endure the contrast. My weaknesses help me to understand the weaknesses of others.

Who can understand his errors? cleanse thou me from secret faults.

Psalms 19:12

Everything needed to make a saint is in the home.

I shall endeavor not to look back unless it is to derive useful lessons from past errors and for the purpose of profiting by dearly bought experience.

A good person is influenced by God Himself.

Goodness and Kindness

Other foundation can no man lay than that is laid, which is Jesus Christ.

1 Corinthians 3:11

You're wanted! Person with the right attitude, with high Christian ideals, and with good moral habits—there's plenty of room at the top for those who will pay the price. Merchants want you to sweep out the store for a few years and ultimately to take charge of it. Newspapers want you to start at the bottom and work to the roomy space on top. You are wanted everywhere—in the law, in medical practice, in the bank, and to run public works. The people who pay big salaries are looking for you. The people want you for a judge in the court, a member of Congress, and a senator and a President, and the nicest person in the world wants you as a spouse.

An honest person is the noblest work of God.

I am blessed if I have a tender conscience. I can discern what is evil and avoid it. If I do not let my conscience become hardened, I can shun evil as quickly as the eyelid closes itself against a speck of dust.

A straight line is shortest in morals as well as in geometry.

The path of falsehood is so perplexing we finally become entangled in our own snares.

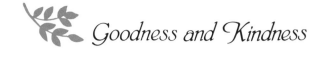

Goodness and Kindness

If I keep my conscience pure, I shall have a continual Christmas.

I must learn what is true in order to do what is right.

My conscience is a safe guide if I keep myself enlightened by the Word of God.

Conscience is the voice of the soul.

Genuine goodness has love for its essence, humility for its clothing, the good of others as its employment, and the honor of God as its end.

There will be a golden age only when golden hearts are beating in it. The religion of Christ reaches and changes the heart, which no other religion does.

Sanctify yourselves therefore, and be ye holy: for I am the Lord your God. And ye shall keep my statutes, and do them: I am the Lord which sanctify you.

Leviticus 20:7-8

The head truly enlightened will presently have a wonderful influence in purifying the heart.

I have no right to do as I please unless I please to do right.

The only solution to human problems is a change in the hearts of people.

Do unto others as though you were the others.

Goodness and Kindness

May I always possess firmness and virtue enough
to maintain what is the most enviable of all titles —
an honest person.

Deserve honor by your own virtue.

> Be like Jesus — this my song,
> In the home and in the throng,
> Be like Jesus all day long:
> I would be like Jesus!

But we all, with open face beholding as in a glass
the glory of the Lord, are changed into the same
image from glory to glory, even as by the Spirit of
the Lord.

II Corinthians 3:18

No better heritage can a father bequeath to his
children than a good name.

Instead of spending so much time looking for
wealth to leave to our children, why don't we
secure for them virtuous habits which are worth
more than money?

The best way to preserve democracy is to
deserve it.

True liberty can never interfere with the duties
and rights of others who are doing what
they ought.

Honor is like the eye, which cannot suffer the least
impurity without damage. It is a precious stone, the
price of which is lessened by a single flaw.

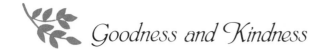

Goodness and Kindness

Here is a good schedule for me to follow:

BEGIN THE DAY WITH GOD
Kneel down to Him in prayer:
Lift up my heart to His abode,
And seek His love to share.

OPEN THE BOOK OF GOD
And read a portion there;
That it may hallow all my thoughts,
And sweeten all my care.

GO THROUGH THE DAY WITH GOD
Whate'er my work may be;
Where'er I am — at home, abroad,
He still is near to me.

CONVERSE IN MIND WITH GOD
My spirit heavenward raise;
Acknowledge every good bestowed,
And offer grateful praise.

LIE DOWN AT NIGHT WITH GOD
Who gives His servants sleep;
And when I tread the vale of death
He will me guard and keep.

Anonymous

Rest in the Lord, and wait patiently for him.

Psalms 37:7

Walking in the
Way of
Patience

 *Patience*

But let patience have her perfect work, that ye may
be perfect and entire, wanting nothing.

James 1:4

This Bible admonition tells me that it is patience
which perfects us. We all need more patience,
though it does seem to me that the more I have, the
more my family wants to use.

The best school of discipline is home. Family life is
God's own method of training the young.

Boys will be boys and boys will grow up to be men.
As the twig is bent, the tree is inclined. Of all the
graces parents need, surely patience heads the list.
If necessary, tell your child a thousand times,
"Close the door, wash your hands, brush your
teeth, study your lessons."

Education does not commence with the alphabet. It
begins with a mother's look, with a father's nod of
approbation, or a sign of reproof; with a sister's
gentle pressure of the hand, or a brother's noble
act of forbearance; with thoughts directed to
beauty, to acts of benevolence, to deeds of virtue,
to the source of all good — to God Himself.

Every word spoken in the hearing of little children
tends toward the formation of character.

There are months (perhaps years) between
seedtime and harvest, and the acorn does not
become an oak in a day.

And thou shalt teach them diligently unto thy
children, and shalt talk of them when thou sittest in
thine house, and when thou walkest by the way,
and when thou liest down, and when thou risest up.

Deuteronomy 6:7

Our daughter was slow in learning the
multiplication tables. We talked the times tables so
much that we would say, "Good–night, darling, how
much is 8 times 6?" We drilled her with most every
question and statement ("Good–morning, princess,
how much is 3 times 8?") until she knew her
"twotems" as she called them, and up to
her twelves.

All fathers, mothers and teachers have the
opportunity to train children.

Patience is active. It is concentrated strength. To
learn to wait is a great secret of success.

Learn to take life just as it blows. Work and trust
and wait.

A great work requires a great and careful training.

God is still trying to teach me that listening is the
most important part of conversation.

The Lord disciplines those whom He loves, and
chastises those whom He receives.

Let us run with patience the race that is set
before us.

Hebrews 12:1

 *Patience*

You cannot put the same shoe on every foot.

We do the difficult immediately — the impossible takes a little longer.

Hurry is good for catching flies.

When an archer misses his mark, he seeks for the cause within himself.

Parents should not expect horse and buggy notions out of jet–age kids.

Housework is something you do which nobody notices unless you don't do it.

Only the best behavior is good enough for daily use in the home.

My neighbor's little boy is confused. Everytime his Mama gets worn out he has to take a nap.

Any woman who is married to a man who thinks he is smarter than his wife is surely married to some smart woman.

When you get to the "end of the rope," tie a knot in it and hang on. This is just another way of saying, "Wait upon the Lord."

Wait on the Lord: be of good courage, and he shall strengthen thine heart: wait, I say, on the Lord.

Psalms 27:14

If Daddy heard us whine, he would say, "What's the matter, whinny-ninny?" We immediately would change our tune.

"I'm sorry, Helen, that you wouldn't let Janet play with your doll. That's being selfish."
"I'm not selfish, I'm just teaching her not to be selfish."

Love grows in us, and we grow in love.

The tallest tree catches the most wind.

The buds swell imperceptibly, without hurry or confusion, as if the short spring days were an eternity.

Experience is the Lord's school and we who are taught by Him usually learn by the mistakes we make. We learn that in ourselves we have no wisdom, and by our slips and falls, we find we have no strength of our own.

Prayer: Dear Lord, remind me often that I will not live long enough to make all the mistakes.

They that wait upon the Lord shall renew their strength; they shall mount up with wings as eagles; they shall run, and not be weary; and they shall walk, and not faint.

Isaiah 40:31

Patience

Like plants and trees, we grow spiritually not only in sunshine, but in rain, wind, lightning, thunder, hail and, yes, even in the earthquake.

In the adversity and darkness of our lives we sometimes see lights which were invisible to us when our lives were all sunshine.

Be ye also patient; stablish your hearts: for the coming of the Lord draweth nigh.

James 5:8

Let patience have her perfect work in all your griefs and trouble.

In time all heaven will break loose.

God upholds us in all our sorrows and is also able to do us good by them.

No contrary wind can last forever.

God permits trials and temptations to come to me only for my own good or for the good of others.

The trying of your faith worketh patience.

James 1:3

The rains will fall, the winds will blow, so we dare not build on the shifting sands.

And therefore will the Lord wait, that he may be
gracious unto you, and therefore will he be exalted,
that he may have mercy upon you: for the Lord is a
God of judgment: blessed are all they that wait
for him.

Isaiah 30:18

> I take with solemn thankfulness
> My burden up, nor ask it less,
> And count it joy that even I
> May suffer, serve, or wait for Thee,
> Whose will be done.

The servant of the Lord must not strive; but be
gentle unto all men, apt to teach, patient.

II Timothy 2:24

> If I have longed for shelter in Thy fold
> When Thou hast given me some fort to hold.
> Dear Lord, forgive.

The Lord will perfect that which concerneth me:
thy mercy, O Lord, endureth for ever.

Psalms 138:8

I practice the presence of God, for I know that He
gives me the very breath with which to praise Him
and that I could not even deny Him unless He gave
me the breath to do so.

 *Patience*

Very often the chip on a person's shoulder is just bark.

Patience is the ability to count down, before blasting off.

He that is slow to anger is better than the mighty; and he that ruleth his spirit than he that taketh a city.

Proverbs 16:32

Patience is the ability to idle your motor when you feel like stripping your gears.

You may not be required to finish the task, but you are not permitted to lay it down.

> Let us, then, be up and doing
> With a heart for any fate;
> Still achieving, still pursuing,
> Learn to labor and to wait.

If we hope for that we see not, then do we with patience wait for it.

Romans 8:25

Patience is bitter, but its fruit is sweet.

Tribulation worketh patience.

Romans 5:3

Every man that striveth for the mastery is temperate in all things.

I Corinthians 9:25

For you have need of endurance, so that you may do the will of God and receive what is promised.

God has a song to teach us, and when we have learned it amid the shadows of affliction, we can sing it forever.

Whatsoever things were written aforetime were written for our learning, that we through patience and comfort of the scriptures might have hope.

Romans 15:4

A man has to do his own growing no matter how tall his father was.

Better is the end of a thing than the beginning thereof: and the patient in spirit is better than the proud in spirit.

Ecclesiastes 7:8

"The good old days" were once called "these trying times."

It is good that a man should both hope and quietly wait for the salvation of the Lord.

Lamentations 3:26

Lead me in thy truth, and teach me: for thou art the God of my salvation; on thee do I wait all the day.

Psalms 25:5

Only I can fill my place in the world.

 *Patience*

I am content, my Father, to know that all my times are in Your hand. *(See Psalms 31:15.)* I cast all my care upon You, and I doubt not that the anchor shall hold.

If I learn to adjust to changing circumstances and remain at peace, then a wind that would blow me off course will instead blow me into port even earlier.

See God in all places, all things, all events at all times.

A heart that worships God alone and trusts Him rises above anxiety.

Complete faith in God puts anxiety to rest.

This shaking world need not shake the Christian's composure.

> Why should this anxious load
> Press down my weary mind?
> I'll hasten to my heavenly Father's throne
> And sweet refreshment find.

Murmur not at the ills you may suffer, but rather thank God for the many mercies and blessings you have received at His hand.

To err is human — and sometimes it is the best thing that could happen to us.

Tomorrow is still untouched.

> Must I be carried to the skies
> On flowery beds of ease,
> While others fought to win the prize,
> And sailed through bloody seas?

Behold, we count them happy which endure. Ye have heard of the patience of Job, and have seen the end of the Lord; that the Lord is very pitiful, and of tender mercy.

James 5:11

> My soul with patience waits
> For Thee, the living Lord:
> My hopes are on Thy promise built,
> Thy never failing Word.

Take me, break me, mould me to the pattern Thou hast planned for me.

In quietness and in confidence shall be your strength.

Isaiah 30:15

If you would suffer patiently the adversities and miseries of this life, be a person of prayer.

Love and wait!

Patience

Anxiety does not empty tomorrow of its worries
and sorrows, but it helps to empty today of
its strength.

I refuse to be disquieted by trifles.

A childlike trust in God is the best preventive and
remedy for anxiety.

> When through the deep waters God calls me
>   to go,
> The rivers of sorrow shall not overflow.
> For He will be with me my trials to bless
> And sanctify to me my deepest distress.
>
> When through fiery trials my pathway
>   shall lie,
> His grace all sufficient shall be my supply.
> The flame shall not hurt me,
> He only designs my dross to consume
> And my gold to refine.
>
> My soul, though all hell should endeavor
>   to shake,
> He'll never, no, never, no never forsake!

Casting all your care upon him; for he careth
for you.

I Peter 5:7

Meekness, temperance: against such there is no law.

Galatians 5:23

Walking in the
Way of
Humility and Temperance

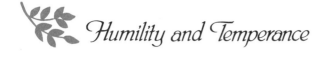

My soul shall make her boast in the Lord: the
humble shall hear thereof, and be glad.

Psalms 34:2

Humility is a lack of boastfulness or show of
conceit.

He hath shewed thee, O man, what is good; and
what doth the Lord require of thee, but to do justly,
and to love mercy, and to walk humbly with thy
God?

Micah 6:8

Humility includes being kind and patient.

> O Hope of every contrite heart,
>   O Joy of all the meek,
> To those who fall, how kind Thou art!
>   How good to those who seek!

Humble yourselves in the sight of the Lord, and he
shall lift you up.

James 4:10

Take a good look at yourself and you will look at
others differently.

Whosoever therefore shall humble himself as this
little child, the same is greatest in the kingdom of
heaven.

Matthew 18:4

Humility is gratitude to God, the Giver of all good
things.

I shall never be deceived more by another than by myself.

If I would reflect upon what a small vacancy my death would leave, I would not be inclined to be too proud of my accomplishments.

God never makes me feel my weakness, but that He may lead me to seek strength from Him.

He giveth power to the faint; and to them that have no might he increaseth strength.

Isaiah 40:29

Just as I am, I come to Thee, with my nothingness, my wants, my sins and my contrition.

If I will, I shall be taught; and if I will apply my mind, I shall be prudent.

And ye shall seek me, and find me, when ye shall search for me with all your heart.

Jeremiah 29:13

Prayer: Dear Lord, help me to simplify everything. May I walk in a plain, simple way and do the duty closest to me, knowing the future is not mine.

I know I am a weak image of my Lord and a poor reflection of His goodness. I also know any mercy I show comes from the Fountain of Mercy and any love I show comes from God who is Love.

May I be willing to help all and also be willing to be helped by all.

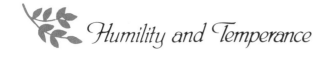

Humility and Temperance

Let me not be wise in my own eyes; let me fear the Lord, and depart from evil.

(See Proverbs 3:7.)

If I fear the Lord, I will prepare my heart and humble myself before Him.

O, may my mind not be corrupted from the simplicity that is in Christ.

(See II Corinthians 11:3.)

Mysteries are revealed unto the meek.

No evil happens to him that fears the Lord; for God will deliver him in temptation.

> As for myself, I try to correct all the errors
> I make;
> That's a high-minded goal, but a true one;
> And I certainly never repeat a mistake—
> No, I somehow come up with a new one.

We can't all be captains—some have to be crew.

Win without boasting—lose without excuse.

To me, to learn meekness is to learn to trust in the Lord with all my heart and lean not to my own understanding.

(See Proverbs 3:5.)

When I come to my senses and find I have so little, I get a taste of humility.

My heart is open to those I love the best, and therefore I cannot close my lips.

Humility and Temperance

True humility makes way for Christ and throws the soul at His feet.

Humility is the genuine proof of Christian virtue. Never fear to admit your mistakes to your children.

The first test of a truly great person is his humility. God walks with the humble; He reveals Himself to the lowly.

The moment I think I am humble is when I have lost my humility. If I am truly humble, I will not think that I am humble.

The meek shall inherit the earth; and shall delight themselves in the abundance of peace.

Psalms 37:11

Life is a long lesson in humility.

I need the understanding of the heart which is better than that of the head.

The first lesson in Christ's school is self-denial.

The very act of faith by which we receive Christ is an act of utter renunciation of self.

Look not at the vices and imperfections of professing Christians. Follow Jesus only as your example and you will learn compassion for those who do not measure up to His standard.

Never underestimate the power of prayer.

For none of us lives to himself, and no man dies to himself.

(See Romans 14:7.)

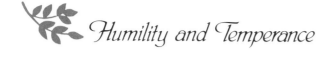

Humility and Temperance

Take my yoke upon you, and learn of me; for I am
meek and lowly in heart: and ye shall find rest unto
your souls. For my yoke is easy, and my burden
is light.

Matthew 11:29-30

O, to be willing to change when wrong and easy to
live with when right!

What a small potato I am, compared with what I
might be!

All I have is loaned to me by God.

The stone which the builders rejected, the same is
become the head of the corner: this is the
Lord's doing.

Matthew 21:42

> O who like Thee so humbly bore
> The scorn, the scoffs of men before;
> So meek, forgiving, God-like high,
> So glorious in humility!
>
> If my duties lowly be,
> Let this suffice — they honor Thee.
>
> O use me, Lord, use even me,
> Just as Thou wilt, and when, and where;
> Until Thy blessed face I see,
> Thy rest, Thy joy, Thy glory share.

O that I would pray as did the psalmist: Search me,
O God, and know my heart: try me, and know my
thoughts: And see if there be any wicked way in
me, and lead me in the way everlasting.

Psalms 139:23-24

Humility and Temperance

May I use well the tools I have.

There is nothing so small but I may honor God by asking His guidance in the matter. Without Him I can do nothing. *(See John 15:5.)* With God all things are possible *(Matthew 19:26).*

Nothing is little in God's service.

Commend not a man for his beauty; neither abhor a man for his appearance. Man looks on the outward appearance, but God looks upon the heart.

(See I Samuel 16:7.)

At ten years of age a boy thinks his father knows a
   great deal.
At fifteen years of age he thinks he knows as much
   as his father.
At age twenty he knows twice as much as
   his father.
At age thirty he may accept advice from his father.
At age forty he begins to think his father knew
   something after all.
At age fifty he begins to seek advice from
   his father.
At age sixty when his father is dead and gone he
   thinks that Dad was just about the smartest
   man that ever lived.

After crosses and losses we become humble
and wise.

Nothing sets a person so much out of the devil's
reach as humility.

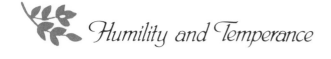

Humility and Temperance

To realize I am a sinner is the first step toward my salvation.

Prayer: Our Father in heaven, look upon the anointed face of Jesus, and look upon us only as found in Him. Look not upon our misusing of Thy grace. Amen.

Abide in me, and I in you. As the branch cannot bear fruit of itself, except it abide in the vine; no more can ye, except ye abide in me. I am the vine, ye are the branches: He that abideth in me, and I in him, the same bringeth forth much fruit: for without me ye can do nothing.

John 15:4,5

The person who lives by himself and for himself is apt to be corrupted by the company he keeps.

Life is a gift from God, and a Christian learns to enjoy it to the highest degree.

As ye have therefore received Christ Jesus the Lord, so walk ye in him: Rooted and built up in him, and stablished in the faith, as ye have been taught, abounding therein with thanksgiving.

Colossians 2:6-7

May each of us take up our tasks for the glory of God. Then we may go to sleep, knowing that no one could have done the job better than we tried to do it this day.

Live virtuously and you will have no regrets.

It is possible to profit by our errors and derive experience from our folly.

Those things without remedy should be without regard. What's done is done, so with Paul, I say, "Forgetting those things which are behind, and reaching forth unto those things which are before, I press toward the mark for the prize of the high calling of God in Christ Jesus."

Philippians 3:13,14

Nothing so well becomes true beauty as simplicity.

Blessed are they which do hunger and thirst after righteousness: for they shall be filled.

Matthew 5:6

God loves us so much that He gave us laws to live by — laws which, if we would obey, would make us happy. He didn't give these laws to us to keep us from doing something, to thwart us, to bind us, to hold us down, but that we might live our lives to the fullest — as a river at flood stage or as a horse running at full gallop, happy, bubbling over. He gave us the Bible that our joy might be full. *(See John 15:11.)* Jesus came that we might have the more abundant life. *(See John 10:10.)* We are so blind to this truth and to the beauty all around us, above us and at our feet. Call that your own which no person can take from you. I may not own an inch of land, but all I see is mine! Life is not a place of entertainment, and youth and health and riches are not the highest attainments of life.

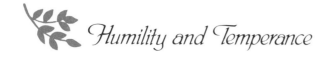
Humility and Temperance

Every man that striveth for the mastery is temperate in all things.

I Corinthians 9:25

Life is a splendid gift. To live my life I must discipline it.

The blossom cannot tell what becomes of its scent, and no person can tell what becomes of the influence and example that roll away from him and go beyond his view.

I cannot run away from my weakness. I must fight it out to victory or perish. If not now, when?

Too much noise deafens us. Too much light blinds us. Standing back too far or up too close prevents our seeing.

Health, beauty, vigor, riches and other good things operate equally as evils to the unjust as they do benefits to the just.

We are creatures of habit. We succeed or we fail as we acquire good habits or bad ones.

Take care to economize in prosperity, you will in adversity.

Gain and income may be temporary and uncertain, but expenses are constant and certain.

Humility and Temperance

No one is poor whose incomings exceed his outgoings.

Saving money soon grows to yield more pleasure than careless spending.

The choicest pleasures of life lie within the ring of moderation.

I do follow the Bible's admonition, "Whatsoever ye do, do it heartily" (Colossians 3:23), when it comes to talking and eating.

If I keep my mouth and tongue, I keep my soul from troubles.

(See Proverbs 21:23.)

Death and life are in the power of the tongue.

Proverbs 18:21

He that refraineth his lips is wise.

Proverbs 10:19

If I will incline my ear unto wisdom, and apply my heart to understanding; if I cry after knowledge, and lift up my voice for understanding; if I seek wisdom like I would search for gold and silver and hidden treasures; then I will understand the fear of the Lord and find the knowledge of God. It is the Lord who gives wisdom; out of His mouth comes knowledge and understanding. When wisdom enters into my heart, and knowledge is pleasant to my soul, then discretion shall preserve me, and understanding shall keep me.

(See Proverbs 2:2-6,10,11.)

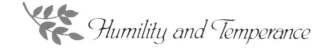

Humility and Temperance

When God would educate a man, He compels him to learn better lessons. He sends him to school to learn the necessities rather than the graces, that by knowing all suffering, he may also know the eternal consolation.

I cannot conquer fate and necessity, but I can yield to them in such a manner as to be greater than if I could.

I may not be able to change my circumstances, but I can change my attitude toward them.

It is true that earth might be fair and all men glad and wise, but it isn't always.

Meekness, temperance: against such there is no law.

Galatians 5:23

I have learned, in whatsoever state I am, therewith to be content. I know both how to be abased, and I know how to abound; every where and in all things I am instructed both to be full and to be hungry, both to abound and to suffer need. I can do all things through Christ which strengtheneth me.

Philippians 4:11-13

Faith is the substance of things hoped for,
the evidence of things not seen.

Hebrews 11:1

Walking in the
Way of
Faith and Hope

 *Faith and Hope*

I shall attempt to express my faith: I thank
God for what I have. I trust God for what I need.

Without faith it is impossible to please God: for he
that comes to Him must believe that He is, and that
He is a rewarder of them that diligently seek Him.

(See Hebrews 11:6.)

This attitude keeps me busy: Mind the present. I
leave tomorrow to God while I pray, "Thy loving,
precious, joyous will be done. Without a but,
without an if, without a limit." Knowing God is in
control of every atom of the universe, I can go
confidently about my daily duties. I am satisfied to
receive the strength I need for the occasion,
moment by moment.

Therefore being justified by faith, we have peace
with God through our Lord Jesus Christ.

Romans 5:1

No claim to superior knowledge can be allowed if it
sets aside what Christ taught.

As many as received Jesus, to them He gave power
to become the sons of God.

(See John 1:12.)

Salvation is God's work — not ours. We merely
accept it or reject it. My lack of acceptance is my
only limitation.

For ye are all the children of God by faith in
Christ Jesus.

Galatians 3:26

I know not how Bethlehem's Babe
Could in the Godhead be;
I only know the manger Child
Has brought God's life to me.

We have access by faith into this grace wherein we
stand, and rejoice in hope of the glory of God.

Romans 5:2

If my problem is big, I turn it over to God, for it will
be small to Him. I fail not to refer all my little
problems to God, knowing they are big to Him if
they disturb me.

It does not bother me that I do not understand and
cannot explain the holy mysteries. I do not fully
understand my husband, my children and
sometimes myself. I cannot expect to understand
God. I am bidden to worship God and believe in
Jesus, my Savior — not to understand.

Don't knock my religion until you have tried it.

Christianity has not failed. It has not been
sufficiently tried.

For by grace we are saved through faith; and not of
ourselves; it is the gift of God.

(See Ephesians 2:8.)

God hath dealt to every man the measure of faith.

Romans 12:3

Am I asking? If so, I shall receive. Am I seeking? If
so, I shall find. Am I knocking? If so, it shall be
opened unto me.

(See Matthew 7:7.)

In everything I must let my request be made known unto God. Of course, He already knows my needs and everything about me, but He said, "Ask, seek, knock."

Sometimes faith must learn a deeper rest, and trust God's silence when He does not speak. There are times when God waits in order that He may be gracious unto us.

(See Isaiah 30:18.)

The real victory of faith is to trust God in the dark.

I doubt not the existence of air just because a strong wind is not always blowing.

I may pray for anything I desire.

I learn to pray as I learn anything else — by regular practice. My faith needs to be exercised.

Now faith is the substance of things hoped for, the evidence of things not seen.

Hebrews 11:1

Truth is on the march and nothing can stop it!

Open your eyes — the whole world is full of God!

God writes the gospel not in the Bible alone, but on trees, and flowers, and clouds, and stars, and on loving faces!

Nature is the living visible garment of God.

Live close to the Word of God. This is the fertile soil from which faith can draw the minerals that make it strong and hardy.

A Bible believer was told that the Red Sea was only six inches deep at that particular time of the year when Pharaoh's army was drowned. "It was a greater miracle than I thought," he exclaimed. "To think Pharaoh and his army were drowned in only six inches of water!"

And Jesus said unto them . . . verily I say unto you, If ye have faith as a grain of mustard seed, ye shall say unto this mountain, Remove hence to yonder place; and it shall remove; and nothing shall be impossible unto you.

Matthew 17:20

Two shoe salesmen went to Africa to open up a new territory for their firm. Three days after their arrival one of them wired home base: "Returning on next plane. Can't sell shoes here. Everybody goes barefoot." Nothing was heard from the other salesman for two weeks. Then came a fat, airmail envelope with this message: Fifty orders enclosed. Prospects unlimited. Nobody here has shoes.

Whatever I do, wherever I am, my hand is in the hand of God.

God shall supply all my needs according to His riches in glory by Christ Jesus.

(See Philippians 4:19.)

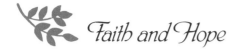

Faith and Hope

I have only to reflect upon how God has cared for me and my family in the past to trust His care for me in the future.

Believe on the Lord Jesus Christ, and thou shalt be saved, and thy house.

Acts 16:31

I fail not to apply and God never fails to supply.

I believe that God does nothing — permits nothing — which I would not do myself if I could see as far as He does.

I pay little attention to my interpretation of providences. I trust God in all instances, whether they seem good or ill, considering every day a good day although some do seem better than others. I see my life as one grand providence!

I consider duties as my business and events as God's business. And I feel God knows His business.

And he said, The things which are impossible with men are possible with God.

Luke 18:27

We cannot see, smell, or touch faith, which is an invisible means of support. It is the unseen things which are eternal. If I can see it, it will pass away. However, the things I see are sufficient for me to believe in the eternal unseen things.

(See II Corinthians 4:18.)

When I am at my wit's end, I find God is there.

He will shield me from suffering or He will send me unfailing strength with which to bear it.

I shall never outgrow my need for prayer, but I must be careful how I pray. If I ask for more patience, love and faith, I may need to be put in the furnace of affliction for God to grant my request.

If I ask God to guide me, He will, provided I completely trust in Him. He will not deem it necessary to show me just how He will guide me, but He will give me light for each day.

The just shall live by faith.

Romans 1:17

If I have God, I lack nothing.

I do not ask to see the distant scene — one step at a time is sufficient for me.

God knows more of all my needs than all my prayers put together have told Him.

I pray "Thy kingdom come," and I work towards that end.

A changeless Christ for a changing world!

May the God of hope fill you with all joy and peace in believing, that you may abound in hope through the power of the Holy Spirit.

(See Romans 15:13.)

67

Faith and Hope

It is good to believe the tangled skein is in the hands of God, who sees the end from the beginning. He shall unravel all.

I know people in whose eyes I may almost read the whole plan of salvation.

I am blessed from having heard the Word of God (and this is how faith comes) from my mother, my father, my teachers and the clergy.

(See Romans 10:17.)

More heroism has been displayed in the home than on the most memorable battlefields of history.

Faith in God hallows and confirms the bond between parents and children. Every act of duty is an act of faith. It is performed in the assurance that God will take care of the consequences.

Pajama-clad child calls out to family, "I'm gonna pray. Anybody want anything?"

A little girl on her knees by her bedside told God the story of Little Red Riding Hood.

A little boy for his prayer said his A B C's. He said that God could make the right words out of the letters.

I leave my prayers with God alone, whose will is wiser than my own.

A faithful man shall abound with blessings.

Proverbs 28:20

Why therefore should I do myself this wrong,
Or others — that I am not always strong;
That I should ever weak or heartless be,
Anxious or troubled, when with me is prayer,
And joy and strength and courage
    are with Thee?

Richard Trent

Jesus became as I am that I may become as He is.

(See II Corinthians 5:21.)

Dear Jesus,
Infinite Wisdom and Infinite Love,
Praying for me to the Father above;
Asking for me what You know is best —
Surely my heart in this knowledge can rest.

Likewise the Spirit also helpeth our infirmities: for
we know not what we should pray for as we ought:
but the Spirit itself maketh intercession for us . . . .
And he that searcheth the hearts knoweth what is
the mind of the Spirit, because he maketh
intercession for the saints according to the will of
God. And we know that all things work together for
good to them that love God, to them who are the
called according to his purpose.

Romans 8:26,27,28

I shall rest content believing that the mind, heart
and soul survive the clay.

And joy of all joys — in my end is my beginning!

Faith and Hope

The joy of the Lord is my strength. *(See Nehemiah 8:10.)* Wonderful is the strength of cheerfulness and its power of endurance.

All heaven is on my side. If God be for me, who can be against me?

(See Romans 8:31.)

What you can do, or dream you can, begin it.
Courage has genius, power and magic in it;
Only engage, and then the mind grows heated.
Begin it and the work will be completed.

Hold up my goings in Thy paths, that my footsteps slip not.

Set in Melior, a typeface
designed by Herman Zapf

Designed and illustrated by
Bob Pantelone